How Banks Create Money
and
Why Governments Should Too

Derryl Hermanutz

How Banks Create Money
and
Why Governments Should Too

ISBN-13: 978-1651225288

An earlier version of this booklet was originally published in late 2019 - early 2020 as a series of articles at Global Economic Intersection (econintersect.com)

Related books by this author:

The Money Problem and How to Fix It (2018)

The Road to Debt Bondage: How Banks Create Unpayable Debt (2018)

A Brief History of Financial Plunder (2020)

Derryl Hermanutz is an independent researcher and writer

Table of Contents

Part 1: The Monetary System

"The study of money, above all other fields in economics, is the one in which complexity is used to disguise truth or to evade truth, not to reveal it. ...The process by which banks create money is so simple that the mind is repelled. Where something so important is involved, a deeper mystery seems only decent." {John K Galbraith, *Money: Whence it Came, Where it Went* (1975)}

"This article explains how the majority of money in the modern economy is created by commercial banks making loans. Money creation in practice differs from some popular misconceptions -- banks do not simply act as intermediaries, lending out deposits that savers place with them, and nor do they 'multiply up' central bank money to create new loans and deposits." {Bank of England, *Money Creation in the Modern Economy* (2014)}

"This means that banks can create book money just by making an accounting entry: according to the Bundesbank's economists, this refutes a popular misconception that banks act simply as intermediaries at the time of lending -- i.e. that banks can only grant credit using funds placed with them previously as deposits by other customers. By the same token, excess central bank reserves are not a necessary precondition for a bank to grant credit (and thus create money)." {Deutsche Bundesbank Eurosystem (*How money is created;* from the English language summary published April 25, 2017 on the Bundesbank's website)}

"There are three main types of money: currency, bank deposits, and central bank reserves. ...Most money in the modern economy is in the form of bank deposits, which are created by commercial banks themselves." {Bank of England, *Money in the Modern Economy* (2014)}

3 different kinds of money

Money is created by the monetary system: the central-commercial banking system.

There are 3 different kinds of money - currency (legal tender money); bank deposits (credit-debt money); central bank reserves (base money) - that are created by 3 different monetary system processes.

Central bank reserves - commercial banks' reserve account balances in their central bank reserve accounts - are banking system money that banks pay each other; not part of the economy's spendable-earnable money supply.

We use currency (the physical banknotes and coins in our pockets); and bank deposits (the spendable *balances* in our bank deposit accounts); as our supply of spendable, investible, savable payments media: our money supply.

Central banks issue the base money supply - reserve account balances and vault cash - to commercial banks.

Commercial banks issue the spendable money supply - deposit account balances and cash withdrawals - to the money-using economy: people, businesses, governments.

Insofar as commercial banks are financial intermediaries, they intermediate between the base money supply issuing central bank and the spendable money supply using economy.

Governments are part of the debt-issuing, money-borrowing, money-using, debt-owing, interest-paying economy; not part of the money issuing banking system.

2 different money supplies

We have 2 different money supplies - the cash money supply in our pockets, and the deposit account money supply in our bank accounts -

that are made of 2 different kinds of money: currency and bank deposits.

We use money as our payments media, to pay each other.

We pay each other currency by direct hand to hand payments of banknotes and coins from buyers of stuff to sellers of the stuff; from money spenders to money earners; from money *payers* to money *payees*.

We pay each other bank deposits - by check, direct deposit, online banking, debit card, etc - within the central-commercial bank-operated *payments system* of debiting payer account balances and crediting payee account balances.

A debit subtracts from a payer's account balance; and the credit equally adds to the payee's account balance. The deposit account "balance" *is the money*: bank deposits.

E.g. when you pay a merchant $100 with your debit card; or pay a $100 utility bill by online banking: your bank debits your deposit account -$100; and the payee's bank credits the payee's deposit account +$100. The money - the $100 deposit account balance - is now in the payee's bank deposit account.

If the payer and payee are both customers of the same commercial bank, then no central bank reserves are involved in the payment. The bank debits the payer's account and credits the payee's account, and the payments system payment is complete.

When we pay bank deposits to a payee who is a customer of a different commercial bank, our bank pays an equal amount of central bank reserves into the payee-bank's central bank reserve account to settle the payment.

Commercial banks debit and credit their customers' deposit account balances to make (clear) the payments.

Central banks debit and credit commercial banks' reserve account balances to settle the payments.

Bank deposits - spendable bank deposit account balances - are not originally created by people depositing cash money in banks.

We do not have cash money "on deposit" in our bank deposit accounts.

We have cash money in our pockets.

We have bank deposits in our bank accounts.

The money supply - the economy's supply of spendable, investible, savable payments media - is originally created in the form of the deposit account money supply: when commercial banks create new bank deposits to fund their bank loans and bond purchases.

Borrowers pay the new deposit account balances to payees.

Then *we* create the spendable cash money supply by making cash withdrawals, and holding our money outside the banking system in the form of the cash money supply in our pockets.

The government or central bank does not print cash money and spend it into circulation.

Currency is sold into the economy by the central-commercial banks.

Commercial banks buy currency from the central bank and pay with debits to their reserve account balances. E.g. the central bank debits your bank's reserve account balance -$100,000, then sends an armored truck delivery of 5000 $20 banknotes to your bank's vault. Your bank stocks its cash drawers and ATMs with the banknotes.

Then we buy the currency from our commercial banks and pay with debits to our deposit account balances. E.g. you slide your debit card into the ATM and punch Withdraw $100. Your bank electronically debits your deposit account balance -$100, and the ATM pays out 5 $20 banknotes. You have converted $100 of the deposit account money (bank deposits) in your bank account, into $100 of cash money (currency) in your pocket.

Commercial banks spend their reserve account balances (base money) settling our payments system payments to payees at different banks. And commercial banks spend their reserve account balances buying currency from the central bank to get vault cash, so our banks can convert our deposit account balances (credit-debt money) into cash withdrawals (legal tender money).

commercial banks and shadow banks

Brokerages, investment banks - and other financial institutions that operate in the savings-funded capital markets financial system - are "shadow banks".

Shadow banks do what most people mistakenly believe commercial banks do: get money from their depositors then lend out and invest their customers' money.

Shadow banks are deposit-*taking* financial intermediaries.

Commercial banks are deposit-*creating* monetary system institutions; *depository* institutions; deposit-*creating* institutions. Commercial banks *create* the form of money they lend: bank deposits - spendable deposit account balances.

The "balance" is a number in a bank account, nothing more. Bank account balances are electronic digits in banking system accounting software: digital money that is paid out (spent) by debiting (subtracting from) payer account balances, and paid in (earned) by crediting (adding to) payee account balances. Most of the debiting and crediting is performed electronically by banking system accounting software; not by bank workers typing on keyboards.

To originally fund (put money in) your brokerage account: you transfer a balance out of your commercial bank deposit account, into your brokerage cash account. Your commercial bank debits your deposit account balance in the amount of the transfer, and your brokerage credits your cash account in the same amount. The balance has been transferred - by a debit and a credit - into your brokerage cash account.

Then you invest your cash balance buying income-paying financial assets. Stocks are dividend-paying *equity* assets: ownership shares in share-issuing business corporations. Bonds (and money market funds) are interest-paying *debt* assets.

When you buy assets, your broker debits the buy money out of your cash account balance; and the asset seller's broker credits the buy money into the seller's cash account balance. The brokers transfer the assets out of the seller's brokerage account into your (buyer's) brokerage account.

The stock issuer pays quarterly (4 times per year) dividends, and the bond issuer pays semi-annual (twice per year) interest. The dividend and interest payments are debited out of the (share-issuing) corporation's or the (bond-issuing) government's bank account balances, and the payments are credited into your cash account balance.

Customers have no direct administrative access to debit and credit our own bank accounts. When we write a check, or make an online banking or debit card payment, we are authorizing our commercial bank to debit the payment amount out of our account; and we are directing the banking system to credit the payee's account.

When we want to buy financial assets, we authorize our broker to debit the buy money out of our cash account, and we direct the seller's broker to credit the buy money into the seller's cash account.

Banks debit and credit their customers' accounts.

Shadow banks debit and credit their customers' cash account balances; in the same way commercial banks debit and credit their customers' deposit account balances; in the same way central banks debit and credit commercial banks' reserve account balances.

assets are not money

When you buy financial assets, you spend your cash account balance paying for your asset purchases.

Your invested money is not "in" the investment (the stocks or bonds or money market funds) that you bought. Your invested money is in the cash account of the asset seller. You *spent* your money (cash balance) buying the income-paying investment assets. You no longer own the money. You now own the assets.

To convert your financial assets into spendable money, you have to sell your assets to somebody who will pay their money to buy your assets. Then you can spend the money.

If nobody who has money is willing to spend their money buying your assets, how much *money* are your assets "worth"?

Assets are not money.

Assets are bought-sold for money.

Money is the liquidity - the payments media - that asset buyers pay to asset sellers. In the capital markets financial system, we use cash account balances as our payments money.

If you have a cash account balance, then you have "money" in your brokerage account. If you have stocks, bonds and money market funds in the account, but no cash balance, then you own assets but you have no money.

Some brokerages now offer "checkable" cash accounts so you can spend the balances directly out of your cash account buying stuff in the "real" economy.

Or you can transfer a balance out of your brokerage cash account, into your commercial bank deposit account, then spend the balance out of your deposit account within the bank-operated payments system.

how commercial banks create (and un-create) the money supply

People, businesses and governments who borrow and spend money that is created by banks are "debtors" who owe the borrowed money back to their banks as payment of their loan account and bond debts.

Commercial banks create the spendable money supply in the form of the deposit account money supply: by making repayable loans of newly created bank deposits to private sector loan account debtors and to government bond debtors.

Making a bank loan or bond purchase creates a linked pair of credits/debts: a new spendable, cashable credit balance (a new bank deposit: e.g. +$1000) in the debtor's bank deposit account; and an equal new interest-bearing repayable debt balance (-$1000) in the debtor's bank loan or bond account.

Debtors spend their new bank loans and bond sale proceeds.

Debtors pay the new credit balances to payees, within the bank-operated payments system.

The new credit balances are debited out of the debtors' bank deposit accounts and credited into the first payees' bank deposit accounts.

That's where the deposit account money supply - the spendable, investible, savable (and cashable) balances in our bank deposit accounts - comes from, in the first place.

Then payees create the spendable cash money supply when we make cash withdrawals and pay with debits to our bank deposit account balances.

But most bank deposits are never cashed out.

Most money never exists in any other form than credit balances in payees' bank deposit accounts.

Debtors owe all of the credit balances back to their banks, as payment of the debtors' loan account and bond debt balances.

Repaying a bank loan; or redeeming a bank-held bond; un-creates - extinguishes; cancels out to $0/$0 - the deposit account credit balance (+$1000) and the loan account or bond debt balance (-$1000) that were created by making the bank loan or bond purchase.

The deposit account money supply - which is about 97% of all money that exists - only exists so long as debtors' debts remain *unpaid*.

But debtors can't pay their loan account and bond *debts* because payees have all the deposit account *money*, which we are *using* as our spendable, investible, savable *money supply*.

The commercial banks' "repayable bank loan and bond purchase" money supply creation monopoly systematically creates *unpayable debts*.

The commercial banks' debt-based money supply creation system creates ever-increasing totals of payees' bank deposit account balances that are owed back to banks as payment of debtors' *unpayable* loan account and bond debt balances; until debtors finally default en masse and the banking system descends into a financial crisis of creditors' uncollectable money that is owed as debtors' unpayable debts.

banking is not the problem

Banking - the business or institution of underwriting loans, allocating the economy's supply of financial credit, and overseeing loan repayments by borrowers - is not the problem.

The modern global buy-sell economy could not function without bankers and banks; digital bank account money; and the globally-integrated, bank-operated electronic payments system.

"Banks" are not the problem.

The banks' *monopoly* of creating the money supply as repayable "loans" is the problem.

Government issuance of debt-free helicopter money is the solution.

monetary system reform proposals

"In short: Nationalize money but do not nationalize banking." {Irving Fisher, *100% Money and the Public Debt* (1936)}

"The Proposal: A reform of the monetary and banking system to eliminate both the private creation or destruction of money... The private creation of money can perhaps best be eliminated by adopting the 100 per cent reserve proposal, thereby separating the depository from the lending function of the banking system." {Milton Friedman, *A Monetary and Fiscal Framework for Economic Stability* (1948)}

All monetary system reformers advocate government issuance of debt-free money to replace, or supplement, the banks' debt-based money issuance.

"Radical" reformers of the Irving Fisher school advocate entirely stripping banks of their money creation privilege, and establishing a 100% government issued money monopoly and 100% reserve banking.

In 2012, two IMF research economists - Michael Kumhof and Jaromir Benes - revived and updated Fisher's proposal in their paper, *The Chicago Plan Revisited.* {Kumhof now works as Senior Research Advisor at the (central) Bank of England.}

In 2011, Dennis Kucinich presented Bill HR2990 - the NEED Act - to the US Congress. The Bill proposed to implement Stephen Zarlenga's American Monetary Institute proposal for conversion from a bank-issued money system to a government-issued money system. The Bill failed.

The Swiss Vollgeld Initiative - that failed in the June 10, 2018 referendum - is of the "radical" persuasion.

ALL radical proposals have totally failed to produce any reform at all.

Do "moderate" reform proposals have a better chance of being understood, accepted, and implemented?

"Moderate" reformers - like Adair Turner, Steve Keen, and me - advocate *some* government money issuance: as much as it takes to paydown the debts to a realistic level;

and then ongoing amounts sufficient to replace the money that payees earn out of the economy's spend-earn stream then hold out of circulation as our accumulations of bank account savings and brokerage account capital.

These ongoing amounts would keep the producer-consumer economy's spend-earn stream "liquid", with enough money-spending in it to enable all the buy-sell transactions that are necessary for businesses to sell all the stuff they produce at money-profitable above-cost prices.

The new debt-free money would replace (or supplement) the present source of consumers' additional spending money: bank loans, overdrafts and credit card debt, that create new spendable money that is owed back to banks as debtors' ever-increasing totals of unpayable household and government debts.

Radical and moderate reformers share the same goal: to fix the monetary system to prevent Collapse; and to keep the money creation system - and the money using economy - functioning.

But no reforms - radical or otherwise - have ever been implemented.

The commercial banks' debt-based money issuance monopoly remains blissfully *un*-reformed, and teetering toward its next Collapse.

Part 2: Central Bank Reserves

synopsis

In Part 1 we saw how commercial banks create the deposit account money supply by making repayable loans of newly created bank deposits to private sector loan account debtors and to government bond debtors. Debtors pay the new deposit account balances to payees within the bank-operated payments system, which creates the economy's deposit account money supply; then payees create the cash money supply when we make cash withdrawals and pay with debits to our deposit account balances.

We saw how commercial banks spend their reserve account balances settling our payments system payments of bank deposits to payees at different banks; and how commercial banks spend their reserve account balances buying currency from the central bank to get vault cash. But we didn't see how reserves are created: how commercial banks get reserve account balances in the first place.

debtors' interest-bearing debts are banks' interest-earning assets

Monetary system banks - commercial banks and central banks - create bank account money to purchase debtors' interest-bearing debts.

Debtors' interest-bearing loan account and bond debts are banks' *interest-earning* assets. Debtors' loan principal repayments are extinguished. Banks earn the interest payments as their income.

Private sector debtors' bank loan payments are "blended" principal + interest payments.

When a debtor makes a loan payment, the bank debits the debtor's deposit account balance and credits the principal repayment amount against the debtor's loan account balance.

Debtors' loan principal payments (deposit account balances) are extinguished, to extinguish an equal amount of the debtors' loan account balances. The loan principal repayment money is cancelled out of existence by a debit.

Banks earn the loan interest payments as their business income. The bank credits the interest payment amount into its own bank account; which is the bank's own spendable bank account money.

Debtors are charged interest based on their *unpaid* debt balances.

Which is why debtors' interest-bearing loan account and bond debt *balances* are banks' *interest-earning* assets.

Government bonds are "term loans". Until the term expires and the bond matures, the government only pays the semi-annual bond interest; none of the loan principal.

When the bond matures and the debt comes due for payment, the government repays the loan principal - the bond face value amount - to the bondholders: the banks and capital markets investors who loaned the government money by purchasing the government's interest-bearing bond debts.

how central bank reserves are created

Commercial banks and central banks both create money - deposit account balances and reserve account balances - to buy assets.

Commercial banks create new spendable money (bank deposits) to buy debtors' new interest-bearing loan account and bond debts (banks' new interest-earning assets) from debtors.

Commercial banks then sell some of the interest-earning debt assets (mainly government bond debts) to the central bank, to get reserves in their reserve accounts.

The central bank pays for its asset purchases by typing numbers - central bank reserves - into the Credits column of the asset selling banks' reserve accounts. The Credits add to the commercial banks' reserve account *balances*.

That's where central bank reserves come from. Base money - reserve account balances - is numbers in commercial banks' reserve accounts. The central bank creates reserve account balances "by typing".

Then commercial banks get the other form of base money - vault cash - by paying with debits to their reserve account balances to buy legal tender currency (banknotes) from the central bank.

The central bank does not directly monetize the government's new debts. The government does not sell new interest-bearing bonds to the central bank, and the central bank does not pay for its asset purchases by typing spendable Credits into the government's central bank account balance.

Commercial banks directly monetize the government's new debts; then central banks monetize some of the commercial banks' interest-earning debt assets when commercial banks sell the bonds to the central bank.

the bond market

Commercial banks "get bonds" by creating new spendable money (bank deposits) to buy new bonds from the bond-issuing government.

Primary dealer commercial banks purchase new issues of Treasury bills, notes, bonds ("bonds") from the government. The bond-buying bank pays for its asset purchase by typing a number - a bank deposit - into the Credits column of the bond-selling government's commercial bank deposit account. The Credit adds to the government's spendable bank deposit account *balance*.

That's where governments get their deficit-spending money. The money is a number in a bank deposit account. Commercial banks create the money "by typing".

The government typically transfers the bond sale Credits out of its commercial bank deposit accounts, into its central bank account, then spends the balances out of its central bank account (usually by check or direct deposit) within the central-commercial bank-operated payments system.

When the government makes a payment: the central bank debits the government's central bank account balance, and the payee's commercial bank credits the payee's commercial bank deposit account balance, in the amount of the payment. The balance has been debited out of the government's bank account and credited into the payee's bank account.

[Like you and me, governments first have to get money before they can spend it. If the government has an insufficient balance to debit (NSF), the government cannot spend money out of its central bank account, or out of its commercial bank accounts. Like you and me, governments are bank customers and money *users*, not money *issuers*.

Governments issue bond debts. Banks issue the money.]

The primary dealer banks typically sell most of the government's new debts into the secondary markets - the capital markets...

where you and I (and our pension funds and insurance companies and mutual funds) buy bonds to hold as interest-earning assets in our brokerage accounts;

and where central banks buy-sell bonds to conduct their interest rate influencing "open market" monetary policy operations;

and where non-primary dealer commercial banks buy bonds;

and where commercial banks sell bonds to the central bank to get reserves in their reserve accounts;

and where shadow banks buy bonds to hold as risk-free collateral against all kinds of derivative credit-debt creation;

and where commercial banks and shadow banks buy bonds to hold as their "near-money" capital.

By a complicated series of transactions that involves debiting and crediting cash account balances, deposit account balances, and reserve account balances...

When we pay our cash account balances to buy bonds in the secondary markets, our invested money actually replaces and extinguishes the new deposit account money that a primary dealer bank had originally created to purchase the bond from the government. When we buy the government's debts in the secondary markets, we indirectly lend our savings to fund the government's deficit spending.

If we buy newly issued bonds via a Treasury Direct program that is administered by our commercial bank, we directly lend our money (deposit account balance) to the government.

In both cases - whether we pay our cash account balance to buy and hold the bond in our brokerage account; or pay a deposit account balance to buy and hold the bond in our commercial bank:

The debtor government pays us (the creditor bondholder) the semi-annual bond interest; and when the bond matures the government pays us back the face value amount of the bond - the "loan principal". The interest payments and bond redemption money are debited out of the government's central bank account and credited into our bank account: our brokerage (shadow bank) cash account; or our commercial bank deposit account.

Bonds (interest-paying debt assets) are by far the biggest asset class* in the capital markets financial system. The bond market is enormous. Stocks (dividend-paying equity assets) are a distant second biggest asset class.

*[Since 2009, stock price inflation has inflated equity asset valuations; which has increased the valuation of stocks relative to bonds.]

Bonds and stocks are dwarfed by derivatives (credit default swaps, interest rate swaps, and more exotic instruments) that are created by shadow banks and their counterparties. But derivatives are more accurately classified as *insurance policies*, that don't payout unless the insured event occurs: a debtor defaults, or an interest rate changes.

Bonds and stocks, by contrast, are income-paying *financial assets* that regularly pay interest income and dividend income to the bondholders and stockholders.

"risk-free" debt assets

"Primary dealer" banks are primary dealers in *government debt*.

Primary dealer commercial banks purchase new bonds directly from the government, then sell the interest-earning debt assets to the central bank, to non-primary dealer commercial banks, and to shadow banks, in the secondary markets.

Government bond debt is considered a "risk-free" banking system assets: free of default risk...

assuming the government can always get money to pay its bond interest - and to redeem its bonds when the debts mature and the loan principal amount comes due for payment - by taxing money from its citizens and businesses;

and by selling the public assets - infrastructure, land, resources - to get money to pay to the creditor banks and investors - the bondholders who loaned the government money by buying the government's debts.

[Private sector debts are banks' risk assets, because people and businesses can and do default on repaying their bank loans.

Under QE (quantitative easing) programs, central banks buy all kinds of risk assets...

like mortgage-backed securities (MBS), which are securitized bundles of debtors' defaulting mortgage loan debts;

and collateralized debt obligation (CDOs), which are securitized bundles of debtors' defaulting car loan debts and student loan debts...

from commercial banks, and pay with newly created money assets: reserve account balances.]

The BIS (Bank for International Settlements) in Basel, Switzerland is the central bankers' central bank, where central bankers harmonize national monetary (money and banking) policies.

Under the Basel capital adequacy protocols, commercial banks must hold liquid capital (their own money) as a percentage of their risk-weighted assets (debtors' interest-paying debts).

Government bond debt is rated at zero risk, so banks can create deposit account balances (deposit liabilities) to buy and hold unlimited amounts of interest-paying government debt on the asset side of their balance sheets.

Bonds are a highly liquid financial asset. If you own bonds and need money, it is usually very easy to sell the bonds to get paid the buyer's money.

Because bonds are so liquid - so easy to sell to get money - banks hold bonds as "near-money" capital on their balance sheets.

During a financial crisis: liquidity evaporates, cash becomes king, and bonds become unsellable.

So if banks need to spend their liquid capital - their own money - to pay their own debts, they can't do it: because instead of holding non-interest paying money balances* they are holding interest-paying financial assets as "near" money.

*[Some central banks now pay fractional percentage interest on commercial banks' "excess" reserve account balances; so even these banks' money assets are "interest-earning" assets.]

Bank deposits are *credit-debt* instruments that commercial banks create to fund their bank loans and bond purchases.

Our deposit account *credit* balances are our banks' deposit liability *debt* balances.

Our bank deposit account balances are our spendable, cashable money assets (deposit account credit balances) that are owed as our banks' payable money liabilities (deposit liability debt balances).

When banks suffer liquidity failure - when banks run out of reserve account balances and vault cash - banks default on *paying* their money liabilities, and our deposit account credit balances no longer "work" as spendable, cashable "money in the bank".

We can't spend our deposit account balance by check, online banking or debit card because our illiquid bank has an insufficient reserve account balance (NSF) for the central bank to debit to settle the payments. So our payment attempts fail. Our deposit account is not debited, and the payee's deposit account is not credited, with the payment. The credit balance is still "in" our bank deposit account; but we can't *spend it.*

We can't cashout our credit balance for payment in the bank's vault cash because our illiquid bank has no cash money "in" its vault or cash drawers or ATMs; and has no reserve account balance to debit to buy more currency from the central bank.

When banks suffer liquidity failure our deposit account credit balances become our banks' *unpayable* deposit liability debt balances.

To prevent banking system liquidity failure - to prevent commercial banks from defaulting on paying their deposit liability debts and to keep the deposit account money supply working as "money" - the central bank steps in and creates new reserve account balances (liquidity; base money) to buy the government's "risk-free" bonds from the commercial banks.

Government-issued bonds are the "risk-free" interest-earning debt assets that underpin the central-commercial banks' entire debt-based "fractionally reserve-backed" deposit account money supply creation monopoly.

Bonds comprise the main financial asset class - and provide the stable base of "risk-free" collateral assets - for the shadow banking system.

The banking system - the central-commercial bank monetary system; and the shadow bank financial system - is built on a foundation of government-issued debt, not government-issued money.

Part 3: Debt-Free Helicopter Money

Ben Franklin's Pennsylvania colony issued its own debt-free scrip money. The colonial government simply printed paper scrip and spent it paying for whatever the government needed.

People and businesses who sold stuff to the government were paid the new money, which provided the private sector economy with a supply of debt-free government-issued money to use.

Nobody owed the money "back" to anybody else, because the money wasn't issued as loans, so it was not owed back to the money issuer as payment of borrowers' debts.

The "debt-free" scrip circulated as payments money in the colony's buy-sell economy. The colonists could spend, invest, or save the government-issued money they earned.

Saving - earning money then holding it out of circulation instead of re-spending it - did not starve debtors of debt repayment money: because banks didn't create the money as loans, so debtors didn't owe *the money supply* back to banks as payment of their loan account debts.

The money-issuing government did not *debt-finance* its spending by issuing bond debts to borrow money that is created by banks (which burdens taxpayers with never-ending bond interest payments on their government's ever-growing bond debts).

The government did not *tax-fund* its spending by taking money from its citizens and businesses.

The government *money-funded* its spending by *creating* the money it spent.

The colony's buy-sell economy flourished with its sufficient - but not excessive - supply of government issued debt-free "helicopter money".

Abraham Lincoln's Civil War government printed and spent $450 million of United States Notes - greenbacks: legal tender paper currency issued by the US Treasury; which prevented adding $450 million to the US National Debt if Lincoln had issued $450 million of US Treasury *debt* and sold it to commercial banks to borrow bank-issued money to fund the North's Civil War spending.

The South printed their own debt-free graybacks for the same reason: to avoid paying the banks' ruinous 24-36% interest for loans of bank deposits ("check-book money") that the banks created by printing numbers in accounting ledgers; and banknotes (paper cash money) that commercial banks used to print themselves. {Central banks now issue all the paper banknotes.}

$450 million was a lot of money, and would have been a lot of additional debt, in the 1860s.

Total US Treasury debt before the Civil War was only $90 million.

Despite Lincoln's issuance of $450 million of debt-free "helicopter money" to fund some of the North's Civil War spending, total US Treasury debt after the Civil war was $2.7 billion. Which is a 30X increase in US public debt over the 4 years (April 12, 1861 to May 9, 1865) of the Civil War.

The debt is *never* paid down.

A *permanent* 5-10X increase in total public debt is typical of bond debt-financed War spending.

Total US Treasury debt has increased from $0 in 1835 when Andrew Jackson paid off the National Debt, to $90 million before the Civil War and $2.7 billion after the Civil War, to $24 billion during WWI, to $259 billion during WWII, to $1 trillion by 1981, to $9.5 trillion in 2006, to $19 trillion by 2017, to $22 trillion today in late 2019.

Total US Treasury debt has *more than doubled* in just the last 13 years.

If you had told Teddy Roosevelt in 1909 - after US Treasury debt had remained fairly stable at $2.7 billion since 1865 - that total US government bond debt would grow more than 8000 times bigger over the next 110 years (from $2.7 billion in 1909 to $22 trillion in 2019): Roosevelt would have laughed you out of the Oval Office.

Yet, here we are.

And total US private sector debt has grown more than 10,000 times bigger over the same period.

Trillions of government and private sector debt created trillions of deposit account money, which debtors borrowed and spent, and payees now have in our bank accounts.

Paying down the loan account and bond debts un-creates the deposit account money.

Governments don't pay down their total bond debts.

Governments roll over their debts. When bonds mature and governments have to repay the bond face value amount to bondholders, the government doesn't tax-fund its debt payouts by taking money from people and businesses. The government debt-finances its bond redemption payouts.

The government gets the bond redemption money by selling new bonds to commercial banks who create new deposit account money to purchase the government's new interest-bearing debts. Bondholders - who are paid the bond redemption money - reinvest the money buying new bonds, to continue earning the bond interest payments.

Every year the government issues more new bonds than it pays out old bonds, so the National Debt continues increasing year after year, decade after decade, century after century.

Government bond debt increases from $0 to millions to billions to trillions. ...then quadrillions, quintillions, sextillions...

Payees have been paid and still *have* all those millions and billions and trillions of bank deposit account balances that debtors owe back to their banks.

For payees to have more money, debtors have to owe more debts.

For debtors to owe less debts, payees have to have less money.

Within the present central-commercial bank monetary system, there is no mechanism to stop the exponential increase in debt growth, other than mass debtor defaults, banking system failure, and writing off payees' deposit account credit balances to restore solvency to the bankrupt commercial banking system by relieving the banks of their unpayable deposit liability debt balances (like the 1930s).

The private sector as a whole doesn't paydown its total loan account debt, just like the government doesn't paydown its total bond debt.

Some loan account debtors are always earning money out of the economy's spend-earn stream and extinguishing the deposit account money balances to reduce their loan account debt balances. But at the same time, new debtors are borrowing and spending new bank account money into circulation.

When credit-debt growth slows or stalls, not enough new money is being spent into circulation, so old debtors can't earn enough new money to make their bank loan payments. So debtors default en masse, which creates a financial crisis in the banks' debt-based money supply creation (and un-creation) system.

The physical world does not need never-ending *economic* growth: that is impossible on a finite planet.

The financial world needs never-ending *credit-debt* growth to prevent mass debtor defaults, banking system failure, deposit account write-offs, monetary system Collapse, and Debt-Deflation Depression.

Never-ending credit-debt growth is possible by banks typing evermore new pairs of numbers in debtors' bank deposit accounts and bank loan accounts.

The need for never-ending debt growth could be ended, if governments issued debt-free money.

how to create debt-free money

Franklin and Lincoln issued their own debt-free money.

Governments today could - but don't - issue their own debt-free, interest-free money; instead of issuing interest-bearing repayable bond debts to borrow money that is created by commercial banks.

The same governments who passed the money and banking laws that legalized the central-commercial banks' monopoly over national money issuance, can change those laws to enable governments to issue their own money.

No changes to the laws are actually necessary. All that is required is for the government to create - what would effectively be debt-free, interest-free deposit account money - within the existing monetary system; by issuing zero interest perpetual bonds.

Perpetual bonds have no maturity date, so the loan principal amount *never* comes due for payment. At zero interest, there is no interest cost to the bond issuer, ever. Debts that impose no interest cost on the borrower, and that never have to be paid back, are not "real" debts. They are accounting formalities.

Here's how it would work:

The government would issue zero interest perpetual bonds and sell them to commercial banks, who pay for their asset purchases in the usual way: by typing spendable Credits into the government's commercial bank deposit accounts. This creates the new spendable money.

Then the commercial banks would sell the new bonds to the central bank, who would pay for its asset purchases in the usual way: by typing Credits into the bond-selling banks' reserve accounts. This creates 100% reserve-backing for the new deposit account money.

The central bank would hold the perpetual bonds on its own balance sheet *forever*: in perpetuity.

That's it.

New debt-free, interest-free, non-repayable, 100% reserve-backed money has been created in the government's commercial bank deposit accounts. The government can then transfer the balances into its central bank account, or spend the balances directly out of its commercial bank accounts.

a money-funded debt reduction program

Governments could use the new debt-free money to fund a private sector debt reduction program, which would permanently prevent the mass debtor defaults that cause financial crisis and failure of the banks' debt-based money system.

The government pays the new money into every citizen's bank deposit account as a monthly un-earned Money Income. The government's bank debits the government's account balance, and the payees' banks credit the payees' account balances, with the Money Income deposits.

Using the US money system as an example: I suggest the deposits be $1000 per month, credited into the bank account of every citizen 18 years old or over.

A condition of this money-funded debt paydown program is that debtors have to use the new money to paydown their debts, before they can spend, save or invest any of their Money Income.

We do not have direct administrative access to debit and credit our own bank account balances. Banks control their customers' paying money out of our accounts.
The Money Income deposits would be credited into every citizen's bank deposit account, every month. Most loan payments are payable monthly, so the new money matches the old debt payment schedule.

Debtors' banks would simply debit loan payments out of the debtors' bank deposit account balances, and credit the payments against the debtors' loan account balances. The new money (deposit account balance) and the old debt (loan account balance) are cancelled out of existence.

This part of the Money Income deposits is simply extinguished: debited out of existence. Money that does not exist cannot contribute to any kind of spending-driven price inflation.

Up to 1/3 of all student loan debts and car loan debts are delinquent (behind on payments), defaulting, or already defaulted. The debtors can't pay their debts because their earned incomes are barely sufficient to pay their very frugal monthly cost of living spending. After they pay rent and utilities and buy food, they have no money left to make their loan payments.

Adding $1000/month into these debtors' bank deposit accounts would make all these unpayable debts payable. Debtors could pay their debts, and their banks could collect their interest-earning assets.

At $1000/month, it would take 50 months for a student debtor to pay off a $50,000 student loan debt, with their Money Income.

Over a period of months and years, people could pay off their high interest credit card balances and bank overdrafts.

Millions of US households are still struggling to make their mortgage payments on the inflated prices they paid for houses during the mortgage loan-inflated 2000s real estate price bubble. A 2 adult household would receive $2000 per month of un-earned Money Income deposits, which - added to their household earned incomes - is enough to make most of these unpayable mortgage debts, payable.

Over a period of 5 years, a 2 adult household would receive a total of $120,000 of Money Income, all of which would be paid against their mortgage loans.

The program could be continued as long as required, to enable private sector debt paydown to realistic and affordable levels.

would the program cause inflation?

People who don't owe debts could spend, invest, or save their new $1000/month Money Income deposits.

Wealthy people owe little or no debt, already own personal assets like houses and cars, and already earn enough money to pay their cost of living spending. So these people would likely save their Money Income deposits to add to their money wealth and financial security: emergency funds, retirement savings, and the basic financial security of having "money in the bank" - even if you *never* need to spend it.

Money that is being saved is not being spent or invested, so it cannot contribute to any kind of spending-driven price inflation.

And wealthy people would likely transfer balances into their brokerage accounts to invest the money buying income-paying financial assets. Adding new buy money would further inflate the buy-sell prices, and conversely reduce the yields, of stocks and bonds whose prices are already inflated to historic highs by the trillions of new money that was created to debt-finance the 2000s real estate price bubble.

People who sold price-inflated real estate to the mortgage debtors were paid all those new deposit account balances, which they ("we") still have, in our bank accounts (savings) and brokerage accounts (investible capital).

The mortgage debtors owe all those trillions back to their banks.

But the debtors can't earn back and pay back the money, because the payees aren't re-spending the money. We are *keeping it*, as our savings and investible capital.

Saving doesn't fund anything. It just adds to idle balances in bank savings accounts (and adds deposit liabilities on bank balance sheets).

Transferring savings into the savings-funded capital markets (to buy financial assets) adds demand-spending which enables asset owners to ask higher prices to sell their stocks and bonds. Savers pay the inflated asset prices with our part of "the global savings glut".

Low returns on stocks and bonds is better than no returns on bank savings account balances.

And "everybody" would be receiving $1000/month Money Income deposits; $2000/month for a 2 adult household - which more than compensates most investors for ongoing high asset prices and low yields. The Money Income deposits would be tax free.

$2000/month = $24,000/year, which is the equivalent of earning 6% net after tax income on $400,000 of invested household savings.

The Money Incomes that are spent buying consumer goods and services might add to CPI price inflation, which erodes the purchasing power of people's already existing money savings.

If this Money Income program adds 1% to CPI (Consumer Price Index) inflation, then the purchasing power of people's existing savings account balances is being reduced by 1% per year by the program.

If you have $1.2 million in your savings accounts, your money loses $12,000 per year of purchasing power, at 1% CPI inflation. But you get $12,000 per year Money Income deposits added to your bank account balance, so you break even.

Everyone who has more than $1.2 million of "money in the bank" loses more purchasing power than they gain by this program. Everyone who has less than $1.2 million of money savings gains more than they lose.

Almost everybody - including most wealthy people - has less than $1.2 million of money savings. So almost everybody gains more than they lose by this program.

69% of Americans have less than $1000 of "money in the bank".

34% of Americans have $0 savings.

An additional 35% have $1 - $999 of savings.

11% have $1000 - $4999 of savings.

5% have $5000 - $9999 of savings.

Only 15% of Americans have $10,000 or more of "money in the bank".

$10,000 of savings might pay a household's debt payments, bill payments, and other cost of living spending, for 4 months. Then the people have no money.

Almost everybody depends on "having incomes", not on "having money".

Only very rich people have a lot of liquid money: bank account balances and cash in safes. Only very rich people would lose purchasing power, by a monetary-fiscal program that adds equally to everybody's incomes but causes a 1% decrease in the purchasing power of money.

Do rich people actually feel it, actually care, if the price of a bag of Taco chips increases from $2.00 to $2.02?

Very rich people spend a significant amount of their money on very expensive luxury goods (mansions, yachts, art: more accurately called "assets"); but spend a tiny fraction of their money on "everyday" consumer goods and services.

The prices of mansions and yachts are not included in the basket of consumer goods whose prices are included in the CPI numbers. So CPI inflation barely affects this tiny fraction of a percentage of the population who are very rich in money.

Poor people tend to spend most of the money they receive, paying their very modest cost of living spending.

The new Money Incomes that are spent would be paid to the local businesses and landlords who sell goods and services to consumers.

Consumers get the housing, utilities, food and other necessities that they need. Businesses and landlords get the money.

This was Milton Friedman's rationale for his money-funded automatic stabilizer program (presented in his 1948 paper, *A Monetary and Fiscal Framework for Economic Stability*); and for his tax-funded negative income tax (presented in his 1962 book, *Capitalism and Freedom*).

Friedman understood that in a buy-sell for money producer-consumer economy, the money flows "up" to producers/sellers as the goods and services flow down to consumers/buyers.

When consumers have more money to spend, the businesses who sell stuff to consumers earn more money. It is *the same money* that is being paid by consumers (spent) and paid to producers (earned).

The increased consumer spending becomes equally increased business sales revenues and landlord rent collections; which would motivate business investment in the production of more goods and services to sell into the newly demand-rich consumer market; which would motivate the hiring of more workers, and the paying of more earned incomes to workers and suppliers, in a virtuous cycle.

All of these benefits suddenly become possible, simply by government issuance of zero interest perpetual bonds to money fund the "helicopter money" program.

The inflation risk is minimal.

Banks' uncollectable interest-earning assets become collectable, because debtors' unpayable loan account debts become payable, which prevents mass debtor defaults, financial crisis, banking system insolvency that is "resolved" by writing off our deposit account balances to relieve the commercial banking system of its unpayable deposit liability debts, and Debt-Deflation Depression that is caused by writing off catastrophic amounts of the spending-driven economy's spendable deposit account *money supply*.

$1000 per month is not "excessive"

There are about 210 million adult (over 18) US citizens, and each would receive $12,000 per year of Money Income deposits: which totals about $2.5 trillion per year.

About half of the new deposits would be extinguished paying down loan account debts, which leaves $1.25 trillion per year.

About half of that would be saved, or invested in the capital markets buying financial assets, which leaves a little more than $600 billion per year available to be spent on consumption.

Which is about a 3% increase in consumer spending/producer earning, based on 2019 US GDP of $20.5 trillion.

3% is a significant, but not excessive, amount of fiscal stimulus: a 3% increase in consumer spending that becomes a 3% increase in business sales revenues and landlord rent collections. There is no future interest cost or principal repayment cost to taxpayers, because the program is money-funded with debt-free, interest-free helicopter money.

The Money Income debt reduction program generates a number of benefits.

Private sector debts are paid down and solvency is restored to households and to banks' balance sheets.

Consumers have more money to spend buying stuff so businesses earn more money producing and selling the stuff.

Producing and selling more stuff requires hiring more workers and buying more stuff from suppliers, so employment increases and workers and suppliers earn more money.

People can add to their savings and investible capital.

And there is no future repayment cost or interest cost to anybody, ever, because the government money-funded rather than debt-financed the Money Income program. What's not to like?

conclusion

That concludes the basic description of how banks create money and why governments should too.

But I have introduced some terminology - like "balance sheets" and "deposit liabilities" - without explaining what the terms *mean*.

In the monetary and financial world, complexity is the enemy of understanding.

As John K Galbraith observed, the money system has been complexified to the extent that describing all the excruciating details - in 900 page financial economics textbooks written in arcane financial terminology that almost nobody, including the bankers who work within the system, and the academic economists who teach it, actually understands - only serves to obfuscate and conceal the simple underlying realities, not to reveal them.

Banks create the money supply by typing numbers in bank accounts.

"The process by which banks create money is so simple that the mind is repelled."

Which is true. Many people, upon first learning how banks create money, refuse to believe it. Their mind is "repelled".

So instead of believing the simple truth, people believe in "popular misconceptions" about where money comes from...

The government prints the money!

The economy produces the money!

and about what banks do...

Banks are financial intermediaries who get loanable funds from depositors then lend out savers' money to investors!

None of which is true. But many people believe it is true; because the money system has been complexified beyond people's ability to see how the system actually functions; and why it fails.

A monetary system that creates the money supply as repayable loans to debtors, is arithmetically incapable of accommodating money-earners (payees) accumulating the money as our savings and investible capital. Debtors owe it all back. But debtors can't pay it back because payees have all the money.

That logic is so dirt simple that many people simply cannot believe it is true.

But it is.

Nevertheless, many people continue searching for some "deeper mystery" that makes more sense than the reality that the money-using world is held in debt bondage by a money-typing monopoly.

Most people do not know - or refuse to believe - that banks create money out of nothing by lending it into existence.

Textbooks describe - in near-incomprehensible terminology and convoluted detail - how the money and banking system works, but ignore or gloss over its catastrophic built-in failings. So people who study those textbooks never gain a clear view and understanding of the system as a whole: both its workings and failings.

I have been researching monetary systems for a long time. To my knowledge, nobody has ever published a simple but functionally complete description of how the central-commercial banks' debt-based money creation (and un-creation) monopoly works, and why it fails; written in non-technical language that people can actually understand.

This booklet, and my other articles and books, are my attempts to fill that gap. But it's hard to describe simply, a complexified system.

In Parts 1 and 2 - that describe how commercial banks create spendable money and how central banks create base money - I stripped down the system mechanics to the bare minimum that is necessary to describe all the essential pieces and their interactions; without delving into all of the complexifying details and historical consequences.

In Part 3 I described how debt-free helicopter money could fix the banks' debt-based monetary system.

Seeing how the banks' debt-based "repayable bank loan and bond purchase" money supply creation monopoly works, exposes why it fails, and illuminates the technically simple way to fix it:

Add debt-free money into the debt-based money supply.

I will end this booklet here, rather than confuse the issue with details that most people neither need nor want to know.

If you want to venture further down the rabbit hole, I will soon publish the continuation of this booklet - titled, *A Brief History of Financial Plunder*.

For readers who want to conduct further research for themselves, I will include the long-version Bibliography in this short booklet.

Derryl Hermanutz February 12, 2020

Bibliography

Allen, Frederick Lewis; *The Lords of Creation*; (1935); the recently re-published Forbidden Bookshelves edition (2014) added the sub-title, *The History of America's 1%*

American Monetary Institute; www.monetary.org

Bank of England; *Money Creation in the Modern Economy* (2014)

Bank of England; *Money in the Modern Economy* (2014)

Benes, Jaromir and Kumhof, Michael; *The Chicago Plan Revisited* (2012)

Bernanke, Ben; *Deflation: Making Sure "It" Doesn't Happen Here* (Federal Reserve Board; Remarks by Governor Ben S. Bernanke Before the National Economic Club, Washington D.C. November 21, 2002)

Bernays, Edward; *Crystalizing Public Opinion* (1923)

Bernays, Edward; *Propaganda* (1928)

Brown, Ellen; *The Web of Debt: The Shocking Truth About Our Money System And How We Can Break Free* (2007, 2010)

Brown, Ellen; *From Austerity to Prosperity: The Public Bank Solution* (2013)

Brown, Ellen; *Banking on the People: Democratizing Money in the Digital Age*

Butler, Smedley; *War is a Racket* (1935)

Carnegie, Andrew; *Triumphant Democracy: Or, Fifty Years' March of the Republic* (1886)

Dawney, Dr. Emma; *Sovereign Money Initiative* www.vollgeld-initiative.ch/en

Deutsche Bundesbank Eurosystem; *How Money is Created* (2017)

Douglas, CH; *Money and the Price System* (text of a 1935 speech to the King and government of Norway)

Federal Reserve Bank of Chicago; *Modern Money Mechanics: A Workbook on Bank Reserves and Deposit Expansion* (1961-1994)

Ferguson, Niall; *The Ascent of Money: A Financial History of the World* (2008)

Fisher, Irving; *Booms and Depressions* (1932)

Fisher, Irving; *The Debt-Deflation Theory of Great Depressions* (1933)

Fisher, Irving; *100% Money and the Public Debt* (1936)

Friedman, Milton; *A Monetary and Fiscal Framework for Economic Stability* (1948)

Friedman, Milton; *Capitalism and Freedom* (1962)

Galbraith, James K; *The Predator State: How Conservatives Abandoned the Free Market and Why Liberals Should Too* (2008)

Galbraith, John K; *The Affluent Society* (1958)

Galbraith, John K; *The New Industrial State* (1967)

Galbraith, John K; *Money: Whence It Came, Where It Wen*t (1975)

Herman, Edward S, and Chomsky, Noam; *Manufacturing Consent: The Political Economy of the Mass Media* (1988)

Hoenig, Thomas; *Too Big Has Failed* (2009)

Hudson, Michael; one of Hudson's recent books is *J is For Junk Economics: A Guide to Reality in an Age of Deception* (2017)

Keen, Steve; *Debunking Economics: The Naked Emperor Dethroned?* (2001, 2011)

Keen, Steve; *Can we avoid another financial crisis?* (2017)

King, Mervyn; *The End of Alchemy: Money, Banking, and the Future of the Global Economy* (2016)

Korten, David; *When Corporations Rule the World* (1995)

Kucinich, Dennis and Zarlenga, Stephen (American Monetary Institute); *Bill HR 2990, The NEED Act* (2011)

Lippman, Walter; *Public Opinion* (1921)

List, Friedrich; *The National System of Political Economy* (1841)

Mehrling, Perry; *The Global Credit Crisis, and Policy Response* (2009)

Mill, John Stuart; *Principles of Political Economy* (1848)

Mills, C. Wright; *The Power Elite* (1956)

Minsky, Hyman; *Can "It" Happen Again? Essays on Instability and Finance* (1982)

Minsky, Hyman; *Stabilizing An Unstable Economy* (1986)

Pettigrew, Richard Franklin; *Triumphant Plutocracy: The Story of American Public Life from 1870 to 1920* (1922)

Piketty, Thomas; *Capital in the Twenty-First Century* (2013)

Polanyi, Karl; *The Great Transformation: The Political and Economic Origins of our Time* (1944)

Positive Money; positivemoney.org

Public Banking Institute; publicbankinginstitute.org

Ricardo, David; *Principles of Political Economy and Taxation* (1817)

Shearer, Chant, Bond; *Economics of the Canadian Financial System: Theory, Policy and Institutions*; Third Edition (1995)

Smith, Adam; *An Inquiry into the Nature and Causes of the Wealth of Nations* (1776)

Turner, Adair; *Debt, Money and Mephistopheles: How Do We Get Out Of This Mess?* (2011)

Turner, Adair; *Between Debt and the Devil: Money, Credit, and Fixing Global Finance* (2016)

Twain, Mark; and Warner, Charles Dudley, *The Gilded Age* (1873)

Varoufakis, Yanis; *Adults in the Room: My Battle with the European and American Deep Establishment* (2017)

Waldman, Steve Randy; *the negative un-natural rate of interest* (2011)

Zarlenga, Stephen; *The Lost Science of Money: The Myth of Money - The Story of Power* (2002)